THE BIG BOOK OF ISRAEL FACTS

AN EDUCATIONAL COUNTRY TRAVEL PICTURE BOOK FOR KIDS ABOUT HISTORY, DESTINATION PLACES, ANIMALS AND MANY MORE

Copyright @2023 James K. Mahi

Israel is a small country in the Middle East, located on the eastern shore of the Mediterranean Sea.

The official languages of Israel are Hebrew and Arabic.

Jerusalem is the capital city of Israel and is considered a holy city by Jews, Christians, and Muslims.

Tel Aviv is the largest city in Israel and is known for its nightlife, beaches, and modern architecture.

Israel is known as the "Startup Nation" due to its high number of tech startups per capita.

The Dead Sea, located between Israel and Jordan, is the lowest point on Earth and has the highest salt concentration of any body of water in the world.

Israel is the only country in the world with a majority Jewish population.

The Western Wall in Jerusalem is one of the holiest sites in Judaism.

Israel has a diverse landscape, ranging from mountains to deserts to beaches.

Israel is the only country in the world where the majority of the population is Jewish.

The Israel Museum in Jerusalem is home to the Dead Sea Scrolls, the oldest known biblical manuscripts.

Israel is one of the world's leading producers of oranges and avocados.

Haifa is a port city in northern Israel and is home to the Baha'i Gardens, a UNESCO World Heritage Site.

The Yad Vashem Holocaust Memorial in Jerusalem is a museum dedicated to remembering the victims of the Holocaust.

Israel has a Mediterranean climate with hot, dry summers and mild winters.

Eilat is a resort town located on the Red Sea and is known for its coral reefs and underwater marine life.

Israel is home to several UNESCO World Heritage Sites, including Masada, a fortress built by King Herod in the first century BCE.

The Israeli shekel is the official currency of Israel.

The Israel Defense Forces is one of the most powerful militaries in the world.

The Knesset is the Israeli parliament and is located in Jerusalem.

Israel is a secular democracy with freedom of religion.

The Bahá'í Faith has its spiritual and administrative center in Haifa, Israel.

Israel has a high standard of living and is considered a developed country.

A total of 48 earthquakes with a magnitude of four or above have struck within 300 kilometers (186 mi) of Israel in the past 10 years. This comes down to a yearly average of 4 earthquakes per year

The Mediterranean diet, which is known for its health benefits, is based on the traditional cuisine of Israel and other countries in the Mediterranean region.

The Technion–Israel Institute of Technology in Haifa is one of the world's leading science and technology universities.

The city of Acre, located on the Mediterranean coast, has been inhabited for thousands of years and has been ruled by several different civilizations, including the Greeks, Romans, and Ottomans.

Israel has a strong film industry and has produced several award-winning films, including "Waltz with Bashir" and "Foxtrot."

The Hula Valley in northern Israel is a major stopping point for migratory birds and is home to over 500 species of birds.

The Israeli flag features a blue Star of David on a white background.

Israel has a vibrant nightlife scene, with clubs, bars, and restaurants open late into the night.

Ein Gedi: A nature reserve and oasis located in the Judean Desert, famous for its waterfalls and natural pools. It is a popular destination for hikers and nature lovers.

Jaffa is a historic port city in Israel that is now part of the larger city of Tel Aviv. It is known for its picturesque old town, art galleries, and flea market, as well as its role in biblical and cultural history.

Caesarea: An ancient port city located on the Mediterranean coast that was once home to Roman rulers and Herod the Great. Today, it is a popular tourist destination with ancient ruins and a modern amphitheater.

Bethlehem is a Palestinian city located in the West Bank, about 10 kilometers south of Jerusalem. It is known as the birthplace of Jesus and is a major religious site for Christians.

The Old City of Jerusalem: A UNESCO World Heritage Site and home to several religious sites, including the Church of the Holy Sepulchre, the Dome of the Rock, and the Western Wall.

The Sea of Galilee: A freshwater lake in northern Israel that is a popular destination for Christian pilgrims. It is believed to be the location of several miracles performed by Jesus.

The national snack of Israel is Bamba, a peanut butter–flavored snack that is similar to cheese puffs.

Israelis love to dance, and many people take part in group dance sessions called "horas."

In Israel, it is common to see camels crossing the road, especially in the desert areas.

Israelis are very fond of their pets, and there are more dogs per capita in Israel than any other country in the world.

Israelis love to haggle at markets and shops, and bargaining is a common practice.

Israel is home to the world's smallest theater, which only has four seats.

Israelis love hummus, which is a popular dip made from chickpeas, tahini, and other ingredients.

In Israel, it is common to see soldiers carrying weapons, as military service is mandatory for all citizens.

TIPS FOR TRAVELING IN ISRAEL

1. Check travel advisories before booking your trip to ensure that the area you plan to visit is safe.
2. Dress modestly when visiting religious sites.
3. Carry a hat, sunscreen, and plenty of water, especially if you plan to visit outdoor attractions.
4. Respect local customs and traditions, including observing Sabbath rules in religious neighborhoods.
5. Use official taxis or public transportation instead of unlicensed cabs.
6. Keep your passport and valuables in a safe place and be aware of pickpockets in crowded areas.
7. Learn a few basic phrases in Hebrew or Arabic to help communicate with locals.
8. Be aware of security measures when visiting public places, such as shopping malls and tourist attractions.
9. Try local food and drink, including falafel, hummus, and Israeli wine.
10. Be aware of the different customs and practices during Jewish holidays, such as Shabbat (the Jewish Sabbath) and Yom Kippur (the Day of Atonement).

Made in United States
Orlando, FL
19 December 2024

56263067R00024